Keep Fit

Written by Alex Marson

Collins

They put on shorts and tops.

They jog with the coach.

She hangs down.

He zooms high in the air.

She can push off with quick feet.

She turns to hit the mat.

They form an arch.

8

They join in to pull it up.

He darts under.

They keep fit.

Now they cool down.

Keep fit

🐾 Review: After reading 🐾

Use your assessment from hearing the children read to choose any GPCs, words or tricky words that need additional practice.

Read 1: Decoding

- Turn to page 6 and ask: What word could we use instead of **push off**? (e.g. *jump, presses down, goes up*) Repeat for **turns** on page 7. (e.g. *twists, flips, flops*)
  - Ask the children to check their idea by reading the sentence with the new words. Ask: Does it make sense?
- On pages 2 and 3, ask the children to find a word that contains the /or/ sound (***shorts***) and the /oa/ sound (***coach***).
  - Repeat for the /or/ and /ar/ sounds on page 8. (***form, arch***)
- Ask the children to take turns to read a page aloud. Challenge them to sound out words silently. Say: Can you blend in your head when you read the words?

Read 2: Prosody

- Read page 11, reading **darts** with emphasis and expression to represent the movement. Discuss the effect.
- Challenge the children to read pages 3 and 5, emphasising **jog** and **zooms** to link with the actions.

Read 3: Comprehension

- Reread the title and ask the children: What do you do to keep fit? Discuss their ideas and how keeping fit makes them feel.
- Ask: Which parts of the body do the children use? Discuss the different parts of the body the children use for each action.
- Talk about how words can have similar meanings (synonyms). Can the children think of words with similar meanings to replace the following, and to check their ideas make sense?
  page 3 **coach** (e.g. *teacher, trainer*)   page 8 **form** (e.g. *make, create*)

  page 11 **darts** (e.g. *rushes, nips*)
- Turn to pages 14 and 15 and encourage the children to talk about what the children are doing in the pictures. Ask: How does this help them to keep fit?